MOJANG

MINECRAFT™

DEL REY
NEW YORK

Published in the United States by Del Rey, an imprint of Random House,
a division of Penguin Random House LLC, New York.

DEL REY and the HOUSE colophon are registered trademarks of Penguin Random House LLC.

Originally published in hardcover in the United Kingdom by Egmont UK Limited.

ISBN 978-1-9848-2086-0
Ebook ISBN 978-1-9848-2087-7

Printed in China on acid-free paper by RRD Asia Printing Solutions

Written by Stephanie Milton

Illustrations by Ryan Marsh

randomhousebooks.com

2 4 6 8 9 7 5 3 1

First US Edition

Design by Maddox Philpot and Richard Hull

MOJANG

MINECRAFT™
FOR BEGINNERS

CONTENTS

HELLO!

We're so glad you've come to play Minecraft! Picking up this book to start to learn how to play was a great idea. Inside are lots of great guides and tips on how to survive and craft yourself a life in the Overworld.

There's a lot to learn when you're playing Minecraft for the first time, but don't worry! Take a breath, read carefully and don't be afraid to make a few mistakes. Before you know it, you'll be an expert!

Oh, and we're sure you'll enjoy yourself, too!

ALEX WILTSHIRE
THE MOJANG TEAM

WHAT IS MINECRAFT?

Minecraft is a game about mining and placing blocks and going on adventures! It's set in a mysterious world made up of different environments. There are animals and monsters living all over this world. You can choose what kind of adventure you'd like to have – let's take a look at the different ways you can play.

⬢ SINGLE PLAYER OR MULTIPLAYER?

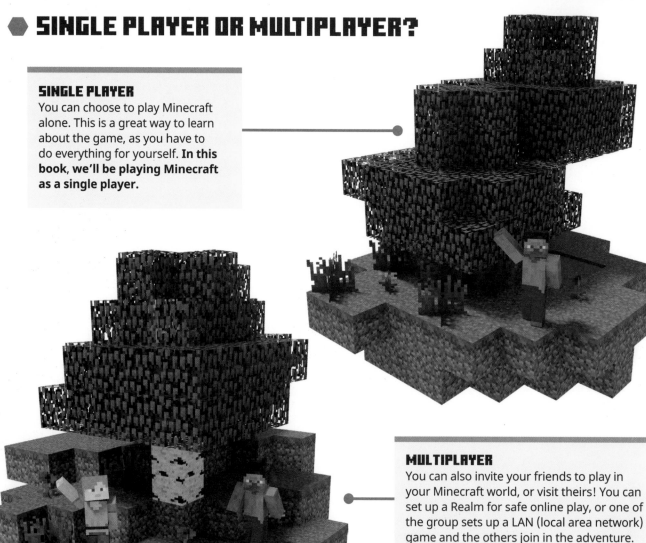

SINGLE PLAYER
You can choose to play Minecraft alone. This is a great way to learn about the game, as you have to do everything for yourself. **In this book, we'll be playing Minecraft as a single player.**

MULTIPLAYER
You can also invite your friends to play in your Minecraft world, or visit theirs! You can set up a Realm for safe online play, or one of the group sets up a LAN (local area network) game and the others join in the adventure.

DID YOU KNOW?

When Minecraft was first created in 2009, the earliest version was called "Cave Game." Later, the name was changed to "Minecraft: Order of the Stone." Finally, it just became "Minecraft." Since its release, the game has sold hundreds of millions of copies.

⬡ SURVIVAL MODE OR CREATIVE MODE?

SURVIVAL MODE

In Survival mode, you'll get to have loads of fun fighting the monsters that hide in the dark. You'll need to mine resources, find food and make a shelter if you want to stay alive. **In this book**, we'll be playing in Survival mode.

DID YOU KNOW?

In Minecraft, time passes 72 times faster than in the real world. Each day is 20 minutes long. Daytime lasts 10 minutes, sunset/dusk lasts 1½ minutes, nighttime lasts 7 minutes and dawn lasts 1½ minutes.

CREATIVE MODE

In Creative mode, no monsters will attack you, and you don't need to eat to stay alive. You'll also have access to as many blocks and items as you like, which means you can build anything you can imagine.

WHICH DEVICE?

You can play Minecraft on lots of different devices. Bedrock Edition is the version of the game you play on Windows 10, Xbox One, Nintendo Switch, mobile devices, Gear VR and Fire TV. People across all these devices can play together. You can also play Minecraft Java Edition on PC or Mac, on Playstation, Xbox 360, Wii U and Nintendo 3DS. **This book covers Bedrock Edition.**

CONTROLS

Have you chosen which Bedrock Edition device you'd like to play on? Great – now you can use these pages to check the basic controls for your device. If you get stuck in the middle of a game, you can come back to these pages for help.

⬡ KEYBOARD AND MOUSE

Use these controls when playing on Windows 10 Edition on your computer.

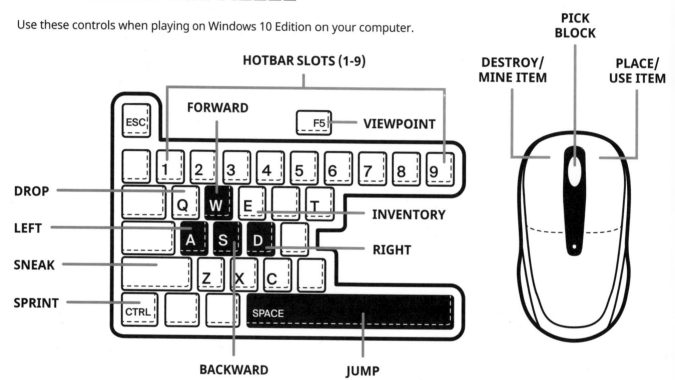

PICK BLOCK

DESTROY/MINE ITEM

PLACE/USE ITEM

HOTBAR SLOTS (1-9)

FORWARD

VIEWPOINT

DROP

LEFT

SNEAK

SPRINT

INVENTORY

RIGHT

BACKWARD

JUMP

⬡ MOBILE DEVICES

Use these controls if you want to play on your phone or tablet.

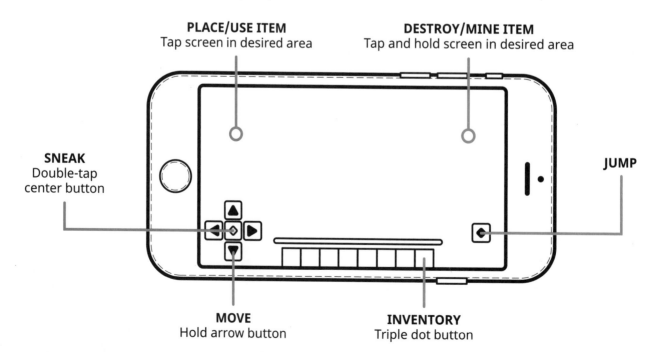

PLACE/USE ITEM
Tap screen in desired area

DESTROY/MINE ITEM
Tap and hold screen in desired area

SNEAK
Double-tap center button

JUMP

MOVE
Hold arrow button

INVENTORY
Triple dot button

XBOX ONE

These are the controls for playing on Xbox One and Fire TV.

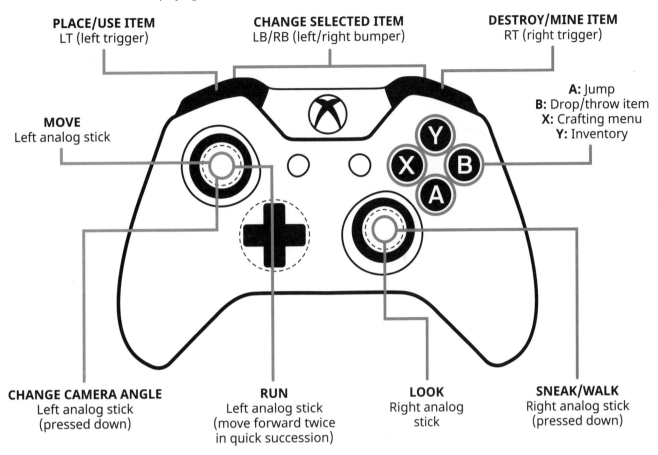

PLACE/USE ITEM
LT (left trigger)

CHANGE SELECTED ITEM
LB/RB (left/right bumper)

DESTROY/MINE ITEM
RT (right trigger)

A: Jump
B: Drop/throw item
X: Crafting menu
Y: Inventory

MOVE
Left analog stick

CHANGE CAMERA ANGLE
Left analog stick
(pressed down)

RUN
Left analog stick
(move forward twice
in quick succession)

LOOK
Right analog
stick

SNEAK/WALK
Right analog stick
(pressed down)

NINTENDO SWITCH

Use these controls when playing on your Nintendo Switch.

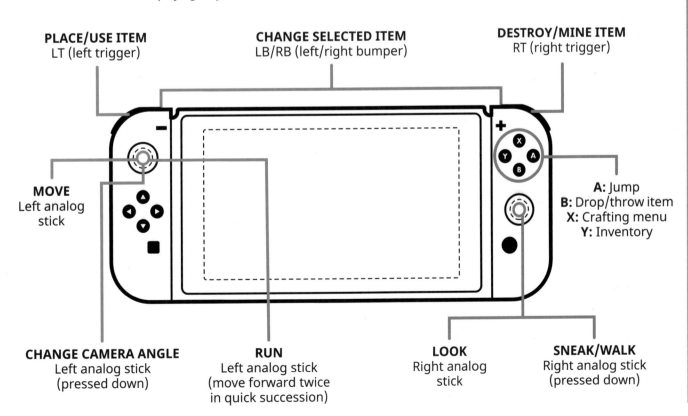

PLACE/USE ITEM
LT (left trigger)

CHANGE SELECTED ITEM
LB/RB (left/right bumper)

DESTROY/MINE ITEM
RT (right trigger)

MOVE
Left analog
stick

A: Jump
B: Drop/throw item
X: Crafting menu
Y: Inventory

CHANGE CAMERA ANGLE
Left analog stick
(pressed down)

RUN
Left analog stick
(move forward twice
in quick succession)

LOOK
Right analog
stick

SNEAK/WALK
Right analog stick
(pressed down)

THIS IS YOU!

Now that you've taken a look at the controls, go ahead and open up Minecraft. But before you hit "play" and start your first game, it's time to choose the character that you'll be playing as in your Minecraft world.

⬡ CHOOSING YOUR CHARACTER

Click on the clothes hanger icon toward the bottom of the screen. There are 2 skins (character designs) for you to choose from: Steve and Alex. Select the character you'd like to play as, then press "confirm." You're now ready to play your first game – turn to page 14 to find out how to begin your first Minecraft adventure!

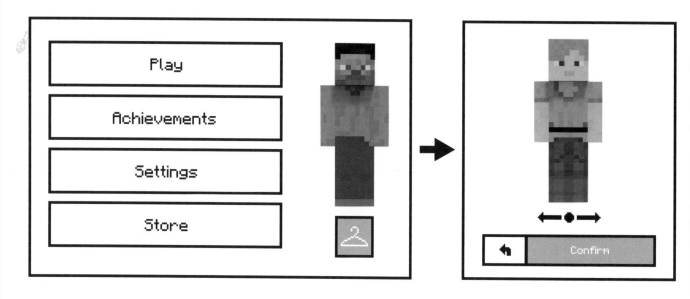

STEVE

ALEX

HEADS-UP DISPLAY

In a game of Minecraft, some important information about your character is displayed on the screen. This information is called your heads-up display (or HUD). Let's take a look at what everything means.

CROSSHAIRS
This little cross helps you to aim at blocks you want to mine, or at monsters you want to hit. It shows the exact point where you will use the tool or item you have in your hand.

HEALTH BAR
Your health bar shows how much life you have left. It's made up of 10 hearts – each heart is worth 2 health points, so you have a total of 20 health points. You lose health points if you don't eat, and if you take damage (e.g., when a monster attacks you). Always keep your health bar as full as you can.

EXPERIENCE
This bar shows you how much experience you've earned so far. You can earn experience points by mining, smelting ores and defeating mobs. Green balls, called experience orbs, will appear and you will automatically collect them if you're standing close enough. Experience adds up to levels.

HOTBAR
These 9 slots are great for storing the items you use most often. There's also a single slot to the left of the hotbar called the off-hand slot. If the hotbar slot you currently have selected is empty and you hit the "use item" button, you will use the item in your off-hand slot.

HUNGER BAR
Your hunger bar is very important, too – it affects your health bar. It's made up of 10 drumsticks – you have a total of 20 hunger points, so each drumstick is worth 2 hunger points. You need to keep it topped up or you will start to lose health points.

YOUR INVENTORY

Your inventory is where you store all the things that you find on your adventures. It has 27 storage slots and a 2 x 2 crafting grid where you can craft simple items. It also has 4 armor slots, where you can equip items of armor to help keep you safe, and an off-hand slot where you can hold a second item in your hands. See pages 8-9 to remind you how to open your inventory on your device.

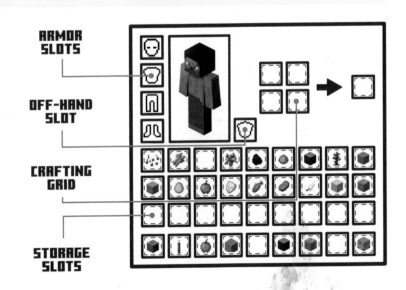

ARMOR SLOTS

OFF-HAND SLOT

CRAFTING GRID

STORAGE SLOTS

MINECRAFT DIMENSIONS

There are three dimensions in Minecraft: the Overworld, the Nether and the End. You'll always begin in the Overworld, and you can travel to the Nether and the End when you're a bit more experienced. Take a quick look at each dimension here.

THE OVERWORLD

This is your home when you first start playing Minecraft. There's lots to explore here – it's infinite! When you start your first game, you'll find yourself in one of 13 different environments (called biomes). You start your game at sea level, which is around 62 blocks above the very bottom of the world, but there's lots going on underground, too. More about that later!

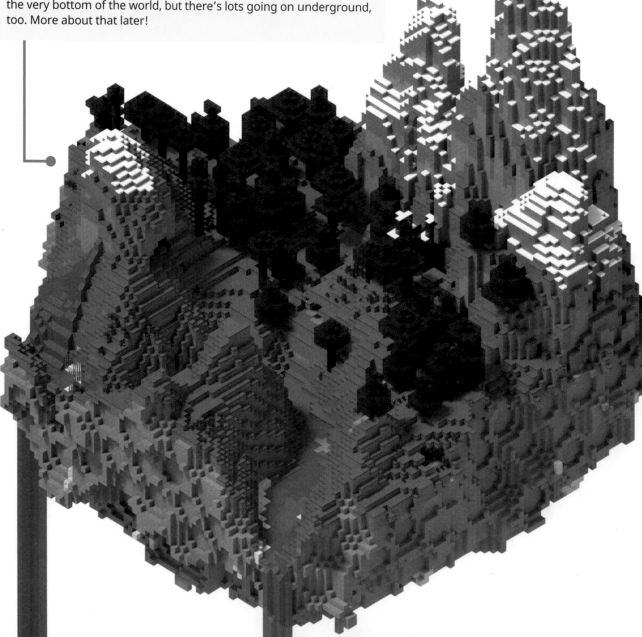

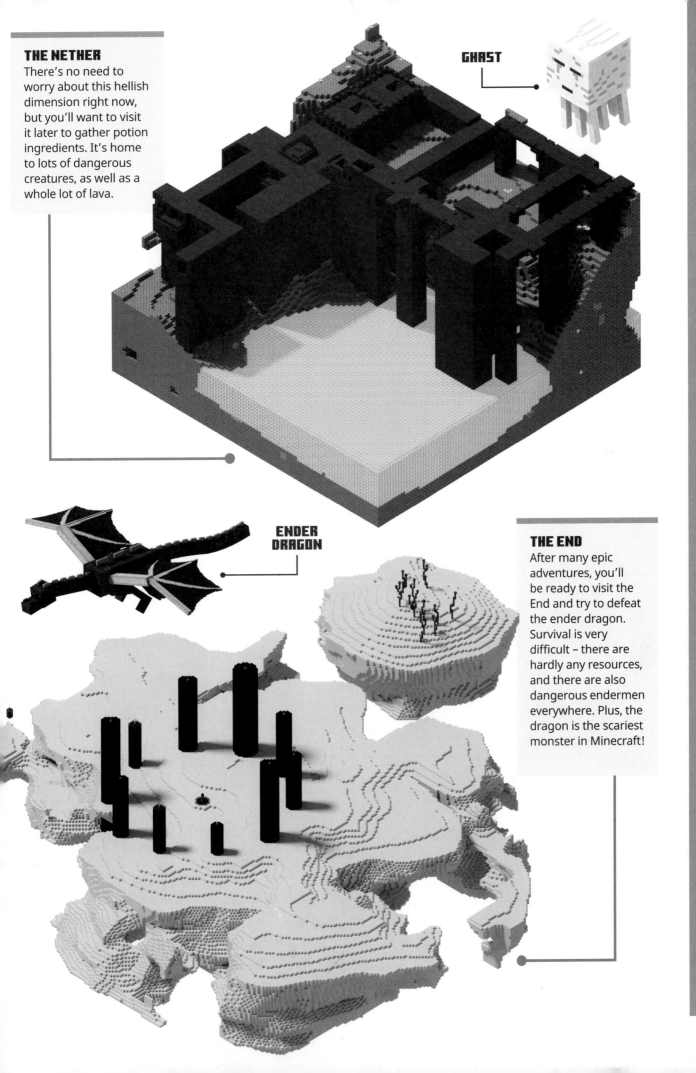

THE NETHER

There's no need to worry about this hellish dimension right now, but you'll want to visit it later to gather potion ingredients. It's home to lots of dangerous creatures, as well as a whole lot of lava.

GHAST

ENDER DRAGON

THE END

After many epic adventures, you'll be ready to visit the End and try to defeat the ender dragon. Survival is very difficult – there are hardly any resources, and there are also dangerous endermen everywhere. Plus, the dragon is the scariest monster in Minecraft!

SPAWNING

The spot where you appear at the start of your game is called your spawn point.
This randomly generated place is very important – what you find at your spawn
point can make the difference between survival and death.

⬡ STARTING YOUR GAME

To start a Survival game in single player, select "Play," "Create New," then "Create New World." Check that the Default
Game Mode is set to Survival. We'd recommend you set the Difficulty to Easy. Now press "Create" and you'll find
yourself in a brand-new, randomly generated Minecraft world. Congratulations – you've just spawned!

Play
Achievements
Settings
Store

➡️

< Create New World

Create

TIP ↗

Young players should ask a parent or a guardian for
help setting up their game.

LUCKY SPAWN
If you're lucky, you'll find yourself in a biome full of
trees, grass, animals and water – all things that are
going to help you survive and thrive. For the best
chance of survival, you should keep creating new
worlds until you can see these things. You're going
to need them!

UNLUCKY SPAWN
If you're really unlucky, you'll find yourself spawning in
a remote or barren area – perhaps on a tiny island in the
middle of the ocean with no resources, or in the middle
of a desert. This is not a good start at all and it's best
to start a new Minecraft world if you find yourself in an
environment like this.

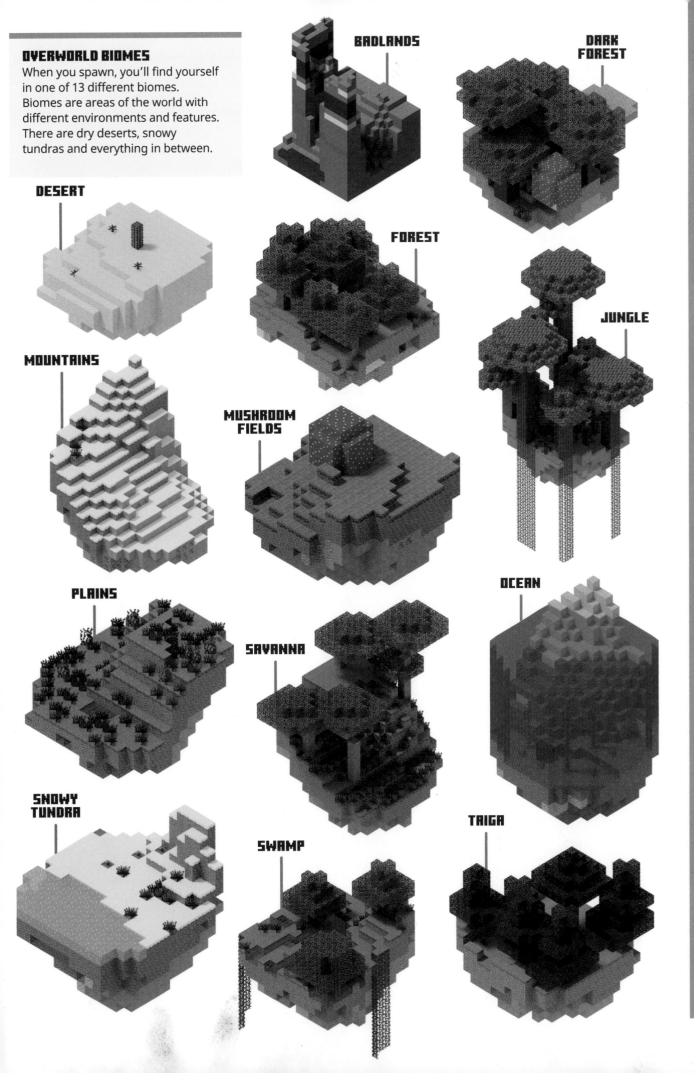

OVERWORLD BIOMES

When you spawn, you'll find yourself in one of 13 different biomes. Biomes are areas of the world with different environments and features. There are dry deserts, snowy tundras and everything in between.

BADLANDS

DARK FOREST

DESERT

FOREST

MOUNTAINS

JUNGLE

MUSHROOM FIELDS

PLAINS

OCEAN

SAVANNA

SNOWY TUNDRA

TAIGA

SWAMP

BLOCKS AND ITEMS

Once you've had a lucky spawn, you can explore and hunt. Everything you see (except for other creatures or players) is a block or an item. Blocks and items can be crafted together to make useful things that will help you survive.

BLOCKS

See that patch of grass over there? It's made from grass blocks. In fact, everything you see placed in the Minecraft world, from water to a torch, is a block. You'll need to break blocks with your hands or with tools to collect them – they'll disappear and be replaced by a smaller version that you can pick up by walking toward it.

DID YOU KNOW?

Different tools work best on different blocks. Sand and gravel will break most quickly if you mine them with a shovel, and wood will break most quickly if you use an axe.

Although your inventory only has 27 storage slots, you can store more than 27 blocks or items. Lots of blocks will stack up to 64 in a single slot. Items like snowballs and eggs will only stack up to 16. Unfortunately, most tools won't stack at all. You'll soon learn what will stack and what won't.

ITEMS

Items can't be placed in the world – they have to be worn, held in your hands or stored in your inventory or a container like a chest. Some items can be found in loot chests that appear naturally in your world. Animals and monsters drop other items when they die.

Things like iron ingots, bones, string, armor and most food sources are items. You need to pick items up from the ground or take them out of containers like chests, then save them in your inventory.

YOUR FIRST DAY

Welcome to your first Minecraft world! There's so much to explore, but we'll get to that later. Right now, you only have 10 minutes of daylight before night falls and the monsters come out. Don't worry – if you follow these steps, you'll be fine!

1 FIND A TREE
Aim at the trunk and hold down the "destroy/mine item" button.

2 COLLECT A BLOCK
After a moment, the block you were aiming at will disappear. You'll see a smaller version of it floating just above the ground. Walk toward it and it will jump into your hotbar.

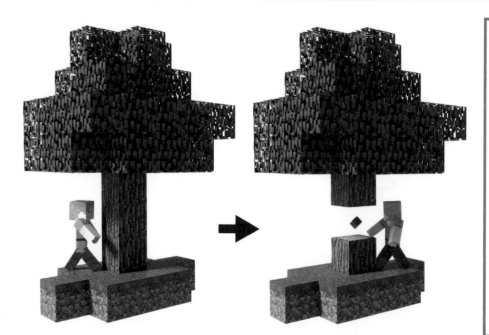

WELL DONE

You've just collected your very first block! In Minecraft, when you collect a block, it's called "mining" a block – even if you aren't in a mine.

KEEP PUNCHING

Let's collect 10 wood blocks. Destroy all the pieces of trunk that you can reach, then find another tree and do the same.

OPEN YOUR INVENTORY

Refer back to pages 8-9 to check how to open your inventory on your device.

CRAFTABLE SECTION

This shows you what you can make with your materials. If something is in a red square, you don't have all the ingredients.

CRAFTING GRID

This 2 x 2 crafting grid is where you can make simple items like torches and sticks before you have a crafting table.

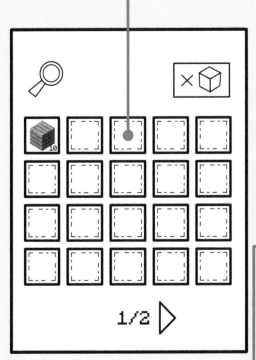

1/2 ▷

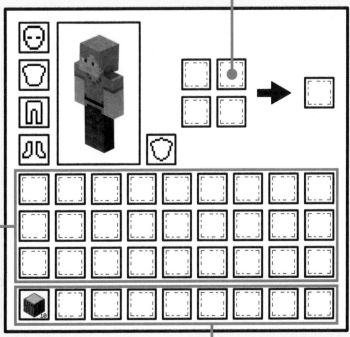

INVENTORY

Use these 27 handy slots for storing the various things you might need when you're exploring, like food and spare weapons.

HOTBAR

These 9 slots are easy to access, which makes them ideal for storing the items you use most often and will need in an emergency.

5 MAKE WOOD PLANKS

Select and drag your wood into the crafting grid. You'll see wood planks appear in the output square. Drag the planks into your inventory until the wood is used up.

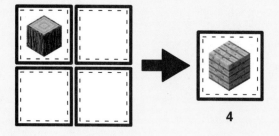

CRAFTING TABLE

Now we're going to make a crafting table – you'll need this to craft more complicated items.

6 MAKE A CRAFTING TABLE

Drag 4 wood planks into the crafting grid. This makes a crafting table. Drag the crafting table out of the output square and into your hotbar.

CRAFTING TABLE RECIPE

PICKAXE

Let's craft a wooden pickaxe. This tool helps you to mine blocks like stone.

7 PLACE YOUR CRAFTING TABLE

Exit your inventory (click on the cross in the top right corner), then select the crafting table in your hotbar and place it on the ground in front of you.

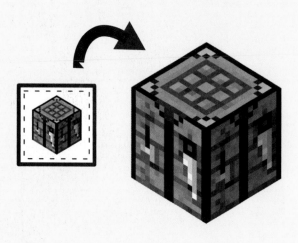

8 OPEN THE CRAFTING TABLE

Select the crafting table and press your "use item" button to open it up. A larger crafting grid will appear – you can use it to craft more complicated items.

CRAFTING GRID

9 CRAFT STICKS

Arrange wood planks in your crafting grid like this to make sticks – these help you to craft tools, weapons and torches. Drag them into your inventory.

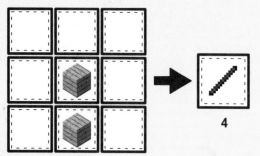

STICKS RECIPE

TIP

Your inventory slots show stacks of blocks with numbers next to them to show the amount in the stack. To break a stack up into individual items (e.g., single planks of wood), select the stack, press the "use item" button and drag the individual items into empty boxes in your inventory.

10

CRAFT A WOODEN PICKAXE

Let's craft a wooden pickaxe – your first tool! Arrange sticks and wood planks as shown below, then drag the pickaxe into your inventory. You need this tool to mine stone.

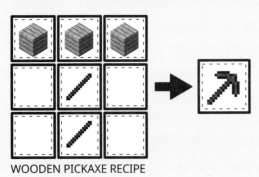

WOODEN PICKAXE RECIPE

WELL DONE

You've just made your very first pickaxe!

11

PICK UP YOUR CRAFTING TABLE

Use your pickaxe to mine your crafting table – you need to find stone next to make stronger tools and weapons, and there may not be any nearby. Drag the pickaxe to one of your hotbar slots, then aim at your crafting table with your crosshairs and hit the "use item" button. Make sure the crafting table has appeared in your inventory before you move on.

12 FIND SOME STONE

You'll often see stone blocks near hills and caves. Aim at a block and hold down the "destroy/mine item" button. After a moment, the block will disappear and a small, mined block of cobblestone will appear floating above the ground. Walk toward it and it will jump into your inventory. Cobblestone looks a lot like stone, but it has lots more cracks.

13 KEEP MINING

Repeat step 12 until you have 20 blocks of cobblestone. You'll need cobblestone for all sorts of crafting recipes, and you can also use it to build a sturdy shelter.

STONE TOOLS AND WEAPONS

Crafting stone tools and weapons enables you to mine ores. They're also useful for defeating animals in order to collect food and are handy for fighting off dangerous monsters. Read on for some essential recipes.

14 CRAFT A STONE PICKAXE

You'll need this tool to mine iron ore. It will also destroy stone more quickly than a wooden pickaxe. Arrange sticks and cobblestone blocks as shown below to craft one.

STONE PICKAXE RECIPE

15 CRAFT A STONE SHOVEL

Now let's craft a stone shovel. Shovels are used to mine blocks like sand and gravel – when used on these blocks, they're quicker than pickaxes. Arrange sticks and cobblestone like this.

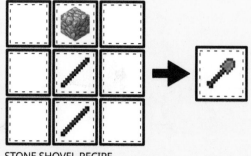

STONE SHOVEL RECIPE

16 CRAFT A STONE AXE

This will help you mine wood more quickly. Arrange sticks and cobblestone like this.

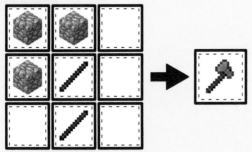

STONE AXE RECIPE

17 CRAFT A STONE SWORD

Your first weapon! Swords can be used to hit monsters and animals, causing them damage and eventually defeating them. Arrange sticks and cobblestone as shown below.

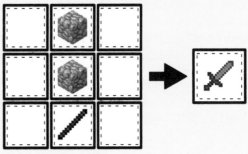

STONE SWORD RECIPE

18 MINE COAL ORE

Once your new sword and tools are saved in your hotbar, you're ready to start looking for coal ore so you can make torches. Coal ore looks like stone, but it has black flecks in it. You can find groups of coal ore blocks in among stone blocks, everywhere from sea level to the bottom of the world. Mine a block of coal ore with your stone pickaxe and it will drop a lump of coal.

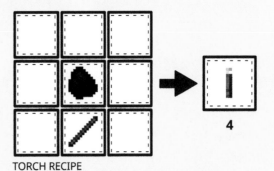

TORCHES

Now let's craft torches – these are essential for helping you see in the dark, at night or underground.

19 CRAFT TORCHES

Craft coal with sticks to make torches. You'll need torches to light up your shelter at night – otherwise monsters will appear.

4

TORCH RECIPE

WELL DONE

You've now made a useful assortment of stone tools and weapons, plus torches to light your way on your Minecraft adventures!

VILLAGES

Now that you have some basic tools, take a quick look around. If you're really lucky, you may see a village nearby. Villages are full of useful items, and you can even camp out in one of the buildings overnight to keep yourself safe from monsters.

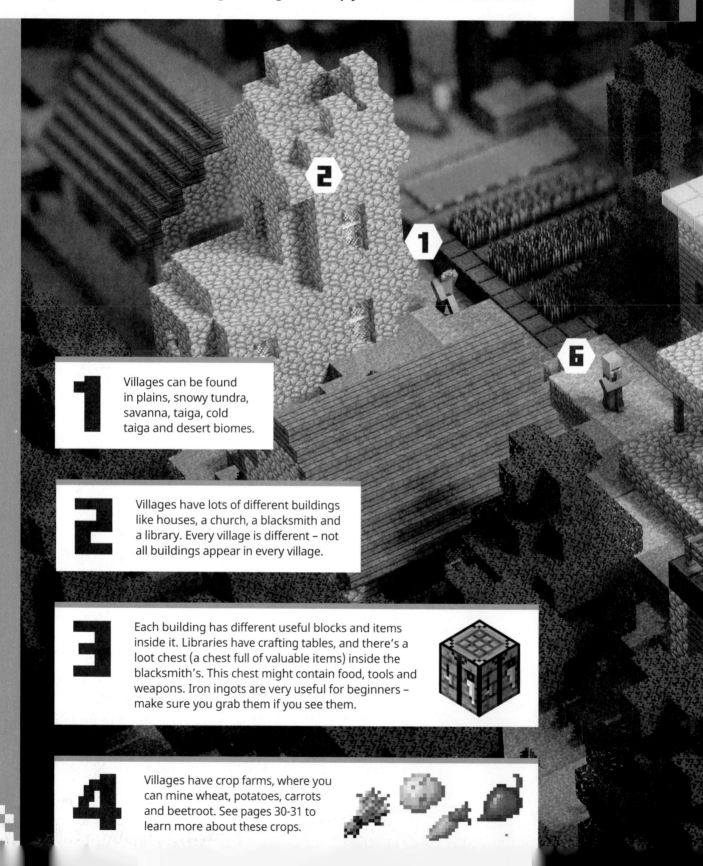

1 Villages can be found in plains, snowy tundra, savanna, taiga, cold taiga and desert biomes.

2 Villages have lots of different buildings like houses, a church, a blacksmith and a library. Every village is different – not all buildings appear in every village.

3 Each building has different useful blocks and items inside it. Libraries have crafting tables, and there's a loot chest (a chest full of valuable items) inside the blacksmith's. This chest might contain food, tools and weapons. Iron ingots are very useful for beginners – make sure you grab them if you see them.

4 Villages have crop farms, where you can mine wheat, potatoes, carrots and beetroot. See pages 30-31 to learn more about these crops.

5 You can mine wood, stone and torches from villages. The villagers won't mind! You can also mine wool from the lampposts. Wool can be used to craft a bed – more about beds on page 35.

6 You'll see villagers hard at work around the village. Don't worry – they won't hurt you.

7 In larger villages you may also see creatures called iron golems. They won't hurt you, either – they're there to protect the villages from night-time zombie attacks.

8 Be careful – sometimes you'll discover a zombie village. Instead of friendly villagers, they're filled with dangerous zombies! You'll know you've stumbled across a zombie village if it's built from moss stone and is covered with cobwebs.

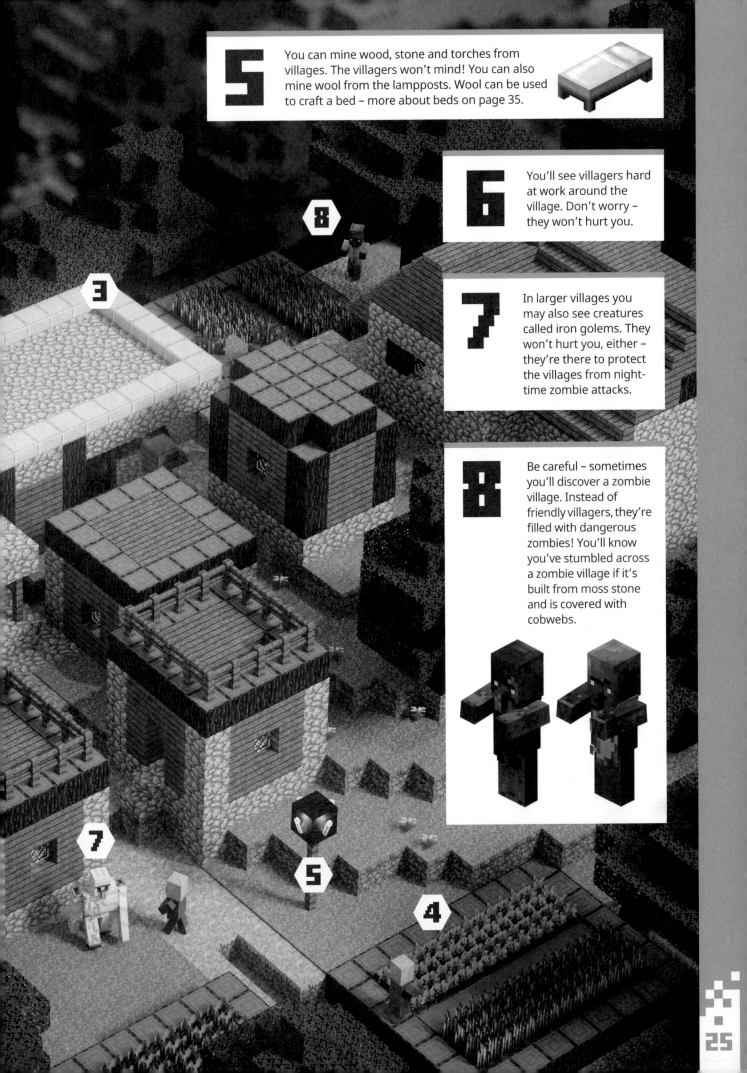

ANIMALS AND MEAT

By now, you will have lost some health and food points. Animal "mobs" – living, moving "mobile" beings – are found in most biomes. Eating their meat is one of the quickest ways to refill your health and food bars.

⬡ DEFEATING ANIMALS

Place your sword in one of your hotbar slots, then aim at an animal with your crosshairs and hit the "use item" button. The animal will try to run away, so be quick! Hit it a few times to defeat it.

⬡ COOKING MEAT

You should cook raw meat before you eat it (see below for how to use a furnace), as cooked meat restores more food points. Chicken must always be cooked – if you eat it raw, you might get food poisoning.

1 CRAFT A FURNACE
Make a furnace from cobblestone using the crafting recipe shown below.

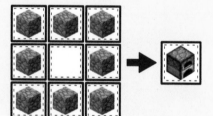

FURNACE RECIPE

2 PLACE YOUR FURNACE
Place your furnace on the ground, then hit the "use item" button.

3 COOKING MEAT
Place coal in the bottom slot – this is the fuel. Place the meat you want to cook in the top slot. When it's cooked, it'll appear in the output slot on the right. Now move it to your inventory.

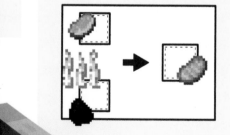

⬡ HOW TO EAT

Food is an item. To eat it, drag it from your inventory into one of your hotbar slots, then select that hotbar slot so you're holding the meat in your hand. Hold down the "use item" button to eat the food, and watch your food bar start to fill up.

CHICKEN

Chickens can be found in grassy areas. They lay eggs every 5-10 minutes, which can be used to bake cakes. You'll see the eggs floating above the ground – just walk up to one and it will jump into your inventory. When defeated, chickens drop 1 raw chicken. Remember, raw chicken can give you food poisoning, so make sure you cook it in your furnace before you eat it.

Raw chicken will restore 3 food points.

Cooked chicken restores 6 food points.

COW

Cows spawn on grass. When defeated, they drop 1-3 raw beef. Cows can also be milked using a bucket; see below. You'll need iron ingots to make the bucket, so turn to page 44 to find out how to mine iron ore and check out page 54 to learn how to turn it into ingots. Milk can be used to craft a cake – see page 31.

Raw beef will restore 3 food points.

Cook raw beef in a furnace to make steak and it will restore 8 food points.

IRON INGOTS
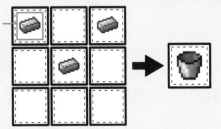
BUCKET RECIPE

MILKING A COW
Find a cow. Place the bucket in your hotbar. Approach the cow, holding your bucket. Press "use item" and watch your bucket fill up with milk!

27

MOOSHROOM

Mooshrooms only spawn in a rare biome called mushroom fields, where the ground is covered in a strange, purple soil called mycelium. These red creatures are a lot like cows, but they have mushrooms on their backs. When defeated, they drop 1-3 raw beef.

Raw beef will restore 3 food points.

Cook raw beef in a furnace to make steak and it will restore 8 food points.

MILKING A MOOSHROOM

You can milk a mooshroom in the same way you milk a cow, and it will give you milk. You can also use a bowl on a mooshroom to get mushroom stew. See page 31 for a bowl recipe and more info on mushroom stew.

PIG

Pigs spawn in grassy areas. You can lure them toward you by carrying a potato, a beetroot or a carrot. When defeated, pigs drop 1-3 raw pork chops.

Raw porkchops will restore 3 food points.

Cooked porkchops will restore 8 food points.

RABBIT

Rabbits spawn in desert, taiga, mega taiga, cold taiga and snowy tundra biomes, as well as in a rare type of forest biome called a flower forest. Their fur is usually the same color as the ground of the biome they're in – white rabbits live in snowy biomes and gold rabbits live in desert biomes. When defeated, they might drop 1 raw rabbit.

 Raw rabbit will restore 3 food points.

 Cooked rabbit will restore 5 food points.

SHEEP

Sheep spawn in grassy areas. Carrying wheat will attract them, within a range of up to 8 blocks. When defeated, they drop 1-2 pieces of raw mutton.

 Raw mutton restores 2 food points.

 Cooked mutton restores 6 food points.

WHAT ELSE CAN I EAT?

If you don't feel like defeating animals just yet, that's OK – there are other things you can eat. Let's take a look at some of the plant-based foods that are all around you and discover what they can be crafted into.

⬡ CROPS IN VILLAGE FARMS

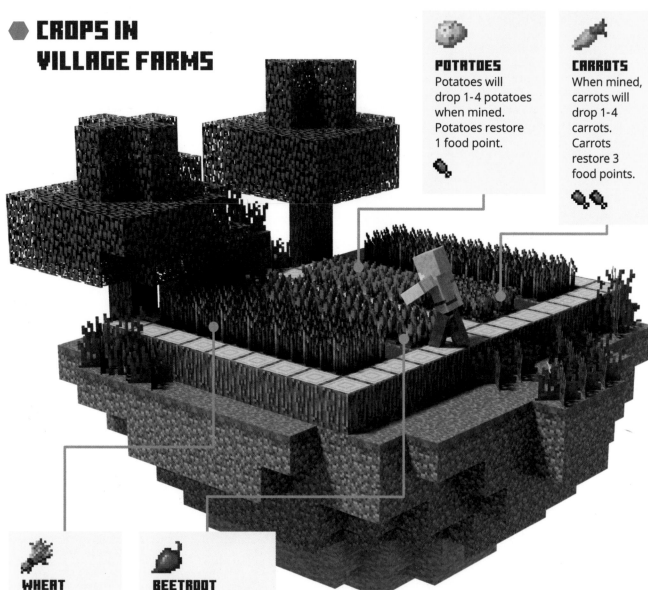

POTATOES
Potatoes will drop 1-4 potatoes when mined. Potatoes restore 1 food point.

CARROTS
When mined, carrots will drop 1-4 carrots. Carrots restore 3 food points.

WHEAT
When mined, wheat will drop 1 wheat and up to 3 seeds that can be planted to grow more wheat. Wheat is used to bake cakes and bread.

BEETROOT
Beetroot will drop 1 beetroot and 0-3 beetroot seeds when mined. You can plant beetroot seeds to grow more beetroot. Beetroot restores 1 food point.

TIP ↗
As well as raiding village farms for crops, remember to look inside any chests that the villagers have made within their buildings, as they'll often use them to store potatoes, carrots, beetroots and apples.

APPLES

Use your hands or any tool to mine the leaves of an oak tree and they may drop apples. Apples restore 4 food points.

MUSHROOMS

Red and brown mushrooms grow on top of blocks in dark areas like roofed forests and caves. You can mine them with your hand or any tool. You can't eat them raw – you'll need to craft them into mushroom stew.

MUSHROOM STEW

Craft a red mushroom and a brown mushroom with a bowl to make mushroom stew. It restores 6 food points.

BOWL RECIPE

MUSHROOM STEW RECIPE

SUGAR CANES

Sugar canes grow near water. When mined, they drop sugar canes that can be crafted into sugar. You can't eat raw sugar – you'll need to craft it into a cake.

PUMPKIN PIE

Pumpkins spawn on grass blocks. Mine one with an axe, then craft with sugar and an egg to make pumpkin pie. A pumpkin pie will restore 8 food points.

BREAD

Bread is crafted from 3 wheat and restores 5 food points.

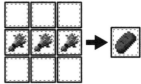

BREAD RECIPE

CAKE

Craft a cake from milk, wheat, sugar and an egg. Place it on top of another block and hit the "use item" button to eat a slice. Each cake has 7 slices, and each slice restores 2 food points.

SUGAR RECIPE

PUMPKIN PIE RECIPE

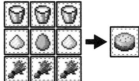

CAKE RECIPE

YOUR FIRST NIGHT

You've gathered as many resources as you can, and now it's getting dark. Dangerous monsters come out at night, so if you haven't found a village to camp out in you'll need to build a shelter – quickly. Here's what to do.

1 Try to find some high ground where you can build a shelter – on top of a hill is a good spot. Being on high ground means you'll be able to see monsters coming and they will never be able to jump on top of you.

TIP

When you die, you respawn at your spawn point. Anything you were wearing, holding or carrying in your inventory will be back at the spot where you died, so you won't have any of your usual equipment. Build your shelter close to your spawn point so you won't have far to go to get back to safety.

2 Build a small, 7 x 7 block shelter using cobblestone. Make it 4 blocks high and add a roof – the roof blocks will float in the air as you build across from wall to wall. Leave a 2 block-high gap at the front for a door. If you can't find any cobblestone, make the shelter from wood or dirt blocks.

3

Craft doors out of wood planks. Place them in your hotbar. Stand outside your shelter, aim at the empty block on the ground in the front wall of your shelter and hit the "use item" button to place a door. Hit the "use item" button again to open and close the door.

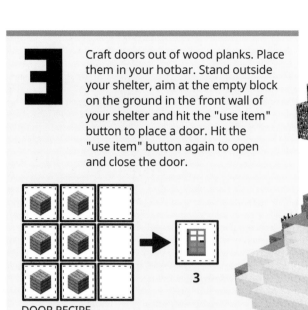

DOOR RECIPE

4

Light up your shelter with torches – this will stop monsters spawning inside. Most dangerous monsters spawn in light levels under 7. Light up the area around your shelter, too, to stop monsters spawning right on your doorstep.

5

Place your crafting table inside your shelter so you can keep crafting during the night.

DID YOU KNOW?

Light is on a scale from 0-15. 0 is total darkness and 15 is full daylight. Different monsters spawn at different light levels – more about that later!

WELL DONE

You're safe inside your newly built shelter and ready for more adventures when the sun rises on your next day in the Overworld!

KEEPING BUSY

Now that you've built a shelter, you should be safe-ish for the night. But there's no time to relax – if you want to survive, you need to use this time to get ready for your second day. Here are some useful tasks that will keep you busy until the morning.

● GET CRAFTING

PREPARE
Craft tools and weapons. Make sure you have lots of torches. Craft a furnace, place it inside your shelter and cook all your meat.

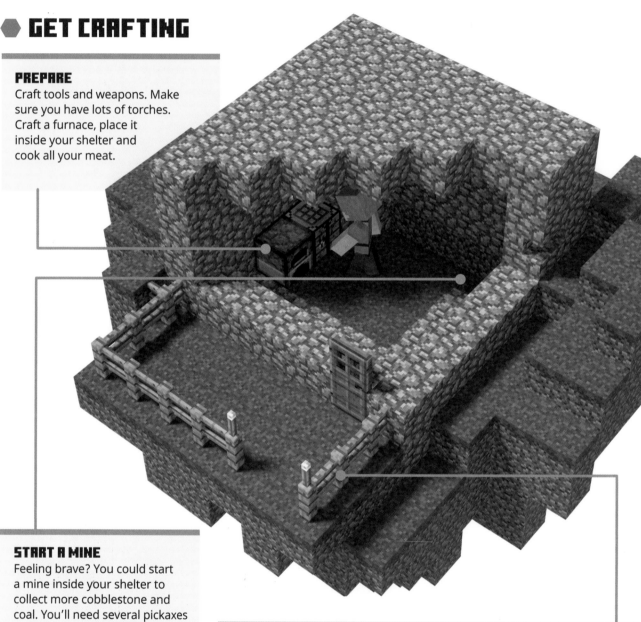

START A MINE
Feeling brave? You could start a mine inside your shelter to collect more cobblestone and coal. You'll need several pickaxes and lots of torches. Start digging down into the ground. Never mine the block under your feet – you don't know what might be waiting for you below. If you mine into a cave, be very careful – caves are full of dangerous monsters, so this might be a good time to stop and fill the hole back in. See pages 48-49 for more mining tips.

CRAFT A FENCE
For added protection against monsters, you can build a fence around your shelter. Create fence blocks using this recipe, then place them next to each other to create a wall of fencing that mobs can't jump over. Wait until morning to place your fence so you don't have to go outside.

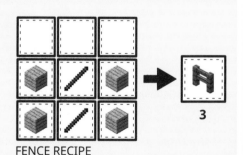

FENCE RECIPE

CRAFT A CHEST

Chests are like inventories – you can store blocks and items inside them when your inventory gets full. They have 27 slots. Keep the things you use most often in your inventory and use your chest to store things you don't need right now. Place 2 chests next to each other on the floor of your shelter and they'll join up to make a large chest, which has 54 slots.

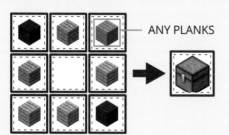

ANY PLANKS

CHEST RECIPE

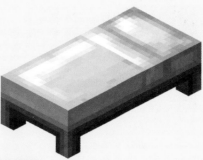

CRAFT A BED

If you found wool in a village (see page 25), you can craft a bed. This is a very useful block – you can sleep in a bed during the night, which means you'll miss all the dangerous monsters and wake up safely in full daylight. Once crafted, place the bed in your shelter, then click the "use item" button while pointing at the bed to sleep in it.

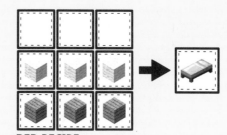

BED RECIPE

DID YOU KNOW?

Villages aren't the only source of wool – sheep also drop wool when defeated.

DID YOU KNOW?

Once you've slept in a bed, that bed becomes your new spawn point. So, if you die, you will reappear by the bed.

THE BAD GUYS

By now, there are probably several scary monsters outside your shelter. Every living, moving creature in Minecraft is called a "mob" (short for "mobile"). Let's meet the most common dangerous mobs that you'll see at night and in dark areas and learn about the useful items they drop when defeated.

CREEPER

BLOCK HEIGHT

------------------- 3

------------- 2

------------- 1

BEHAVIOR
Creepers can be found in all biomes. They spawn at night and in dark areas like caves. Unlike many hostile mobs, they don't disappear during the day.

HOW THEY ATTACK
Don't let their sad faces fool you – they'll creep toward you almost silently (which is why they're called creepers), then hiss for a few seconds before exploding in your face. You won't survive the explosion.

HOW TO DEFEND YOURSELF
• Stay alert and don't let creepers get anywhere near you.
• If a creeper gets close to you, hit it with your sword, then jump back quickly. Keep doing this until it explodes or falls to the ground, defeated.

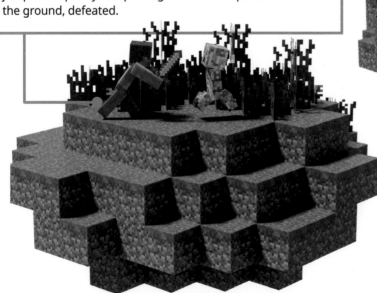

WHAT THEY DROP
If you defeat a creeper before it explodes, it will drop gunpowder. You can use this later to craft an explosive block called TNT.

DROWNED

BLOCK HEIGHT

----------------- 3

----------------- 2

----------------- 1

BEHAVIOR

Mobs known as "drowned" spawn at the bottom of oceans, rivers and swamps. During the night, they can come out of their watery habitats and start to walk about on land, so watch out for them if you're near water.

DID YOU KNOW?

There are two types of dangerous mobs. Hostile mobs will attack you as soon as they see you. Neutral mobs will only attack you in certain conditions.

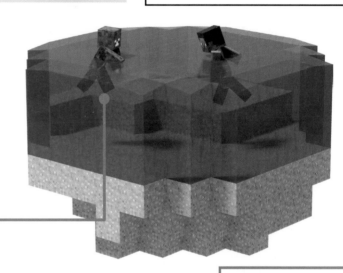

HOW THEY ATTACK

Drowned mobs will hit you with their hands if you get too close, causing damage. Some carry tridents – this is a rare weapon that can be thrown or used to hit players and other mobs.

HOW TO DEFEND YOURSELF

• Hit drowned mobs with your sword and run away.

WHAT THEY DROP

Drowned mobs might drop their tridents. You can't craft tridents, so always grab them if you see them.

ENDERMAN

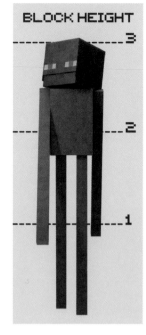

BLOCK HEIGHT

3

2

1

BEHAVIOR

Endermen spawn in small groups of 1-4 in dark areas of the Overworld. They also spawn in much greater numbers in the End dimension. They sometimes carry random blocks that they have picked up along the way, and they also have the ability to teleport.

TIP

If you see any of these bad guys, try to keep out of their way until you're a bit more experienced and have a set of armor!

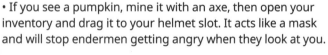

HOW THEY ATTACK

Endermen hate to be stared at – if you look at an enderman, it will become hostile. They will open their mouths, shake with anger and run toward you to hit you.

HOW TO DEFEND YOURSELF

• Get your back up against a wall to stop them teleporting behind you.
• Endermen hate water, so find some shallow water to stand in.
• If you have a bucket, fill it with water and throw it at the enderman.
• If you see a pumpkin, mine it with an axe, then open your inventory and drag it to your helmet slot. It acts like a mask and will stop endermen getting angry when they look at you.

WHAT THEY DROP

Endermen drop ender pearls. You'll need these items later, as they can be used to get to the End dimension.

SKELETON

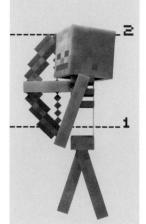

BLOCK HEIGHT

—————————— 3

———— 2

———— 1

BEHAVIOR
Skeletons spawn in dark areas of the Overworld and sometimes in the Nether dimension. There are 2 types: strays, which are only found in icy biomes, and regular skeletons, which are found in all biomes. Both types burn in the sun, so you'll never see them out in full daylight.

HOW TO DEFEND YOURSELF
• If it's daytime, try to lead the skeleton into sunlight.
• Keep moving so it's harder for the skeleton to hit you with its arrows, and try to hit back with your sword if it gets too close.

HOW THEY ATTACK
Skeletons will chase after a player, circle them and shoot them with their bow and arrow. Because they can attack you from a distance, they can be difficult to run away from.

WHAT THEY DROP
Skeletons can drop bones. Bones can be used to tame wolves. Found in taiga biomes, you can tame these animals to be your pets. Wolves will even attack skeletons for you.

SPIDER

BLOCK HEIGHT

---------------3

---------------2

---------------1

BEHAVIOR

Spiders spawn in any area with a light level of 7 or less. Watch out – they can swiftly climb up walls and over obstacles. Spiders will jump around before attacking. When defeated, they flip over and land on their backs (unlike most mobs, which land on their sides).

TIP

Forest biomes spawn the greatest amount of spiders, so avoid forests if you're particularly afraid of them.

HOW THEY ATTACK

Spiders are hostile when the light level is 11 or less, so they'll leave you alone in daylight. In forests, the light level is often below 11, making them hostile by day. Once hostile, they'll continue attacking you, even if it gets light. They leap toward you and bite you to inflict damage.

HOW TO DEFEND YOURSELF

• Hit them with your sword, then step back quickly.
• Try to get to higher ground, so they can't jump on top of you.

WHAT THEY DROP

Spiders drop up to 2 string, which can be crafted with sticks to make a bow.

They may also drop spider eyes, which you use to make potions.

WITCH

BLOCK HEIGHT
------------------- 3

------- 2

------- 1

BEHAVIOR

Witches can spawn anywhere with a light level of 7 or less. They always spawn in witch huts in swamp biomes. When a lightning bolt hits the ground close to a villager, the zapped, unlucky villager turns into a scary witch!

DID YOU KNOW?

Witches can use their helpful potions to breathe underwater, resist fire and move very swiftly. Be extremely careful!

HOW THEY ATTACK

Witches throw harmful splash potions – they splash on the floor and engulf you in their nasty effect. Unfortunately, witches also have healing potions that they will use to heal themselves if you attack them.

HOW TO DEFEND YOURSELF

• Keep your distance so they can't hit you with their splash potions.
• Attack them from a distance if you have a bow and arrow. If you don't, it's best that you run away as quickly as possible.

WHAT THEY DROP

Witches can drop many items, from sugar to empty glass bottles, that can be used to brew potions. They can also drop redstone – a substance that can be used to transmit power. You don't need to worry about these right now, but pick them up because they'll be useful later.

ZOMBIE

BLOCK HEIGHT

---- 3

---- 2

---- 1

BEHAVIOR
Zombies spawn in groups of 4 in light levels of 7 or less. There are 2 types: husks, which can only be found in desert biomes, and regular zombies, which can be found in all biomes. Regular zombies burn in the sun, so you'll never see them out in full daylight.

TIP ↗

Beware of baby zombies – they're rare but deadly. They move faster than normal zombies and can also ride animals.

HOW THEY ATTACK
Zombies will walk slowly toward you with their arms outstretched. They cause you damage when they touch you. They often attack in groups, which makes them difficult to deal with.

HOW TO DEFEND YOURSELF
Try to lead regular zombies into the sunshine if it's daytime. Hit them with your sword, then jump back to avoid their arms.

WHAT THEY DROP
Zombies drop rotten flesh. You can eat it, but it will probably give you food poisoning. There's a very small chance they'll drop iron ingots, carrots and potatoes.

ZOMBIE VILLAGER

BLOCK HEIGHT

.... 3

.... 2

.... 1

BEHAVIOR

Zombie villagers spawn in zombie villages. If a zombie attacks a regular villager in a regular village, they will turn it into a zombie villager.

DID YOU KNOW?

Zombies will pick up and use dropped armor, weapons and tools, which can make them even more dangerous!

HOW THEY ATTACK

Zombie villagers attack in the same way as regular zombies – they move slowly toward you and hit you with their outstretched arms to cause you damage.

HOW TO DEFEND YOURSELF

Hide in one of the village buildings, or get your back up against a wall and fight them off with your sword.

WHAT THEY DROP

Sadly, zombie villagers don't drop anything for you to pick up and use.

ORES

Ores are used to create valuable items that help you survive. The rarest ores are found deep belowground. You need an iron pickaxe to mine most of them (see page 55), so your next task is to find iron ore. The cross-section of a mine below shows you where to look for each ore and what they can be crafted into.

IRON ORE

• Iron ore can be found at all levels, from sea level right down to the bottom of the world.
• You'll find it in patches of up to 8 blocks. Mine it with your stone pickaxe to collect the block.
• Iron can be used to upgrade your tools and weapons and to make useful tools like buckets, shears and a flint and steel.

TIP

Remember, bedrock at the bottom of the world is level 0 and sea level is level 62.

GOLD ORE

• Gold can be used to craft armor, tools and weapons as well as golden apples, clocks and powered rails.
• Gold ore is found in patches of 4-8 blocks at level 32 and under.
• You'll need an iron pickaxe to mine gold ore. Smelt the block in your furnace to make gold ingots (see pages 54-55).

LAPIS LAZULI ORE

• Lapis lazuli is needed to enchant items and can be used as a blue dye.
• The rare ore is found in patches of 1-10 blocks at level 31 and below.
• When mined with a stone or iron pickaxe, each block drops 4-8 pieces of lapis lazuli.

EMERALD ORE

• You can use emeralds to trade with villagers, and 9 emeralds can be crafted into a block of solid emerald.
• Emerald ore is found in single blocks between levels 4–32 in mountain biomes.
• A block of this rare ore drops 1 emerald when you mine it with an iron pickaxe.

DIAMOND ORE

• Diamonds can be used to make Minecraft's strongest tools, weapons and armor.
• You'll also need them to craft enchantment tables and jukeboxes.
• Diamond ore is rare, and you'll only find it at level 16 and below, grouped together in patches of 1-10 blocks.
• When this hard-to-find resource is mined with an iron pickaxe, each block will drop 1 diamond.

REDSTONE ORE

• Redstone ore is found in patches of 4-8 blocks, at level 16 and under.
• When mined with a stone pickaxe, each block drops 4-5 redstone – an item that can be used like a wire to transmit power.
• It can also be used to craft items like clocks, compasses and powered rails.

LET'S GO UNDERGROUND

It's time to get ready for your mission to find iron ore. Mining is risky – it's dark belowground and there are deadly mobs hiding in the caves. If you want to survive, you'll need to take a selection of essential items with you.

WOOD BLOCKS
Carry plenty of wood planks with you on your expedition. There are no trees belowground, and you'll need wood to make tools, weapons and torches.

STONE TOOLS AND WEAPONS
Take a stone sword so you can protect yourself from the monsters. Take at least 2 stone pickaxes – you're going to mine a lot of blocks.

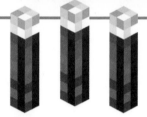

TORCHES
It's very dark underground, and you need to be able to see where you're going! Take at least one stack of torches (64) to light your way.

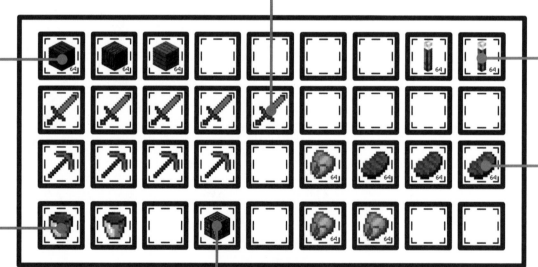

WATER BUCKET
Take a water bucket in case you fall into lava and set yourself on fire. You can use it on yourself to put out the flames, or pour it into a block and step into it.

CRAFTING TABLE
Wherever you go in Minecraft, it's a good idea to take a crafting table with you. You can use it to craft new pickaxes and shovels to replace your old ones.

FOOD
You won't find any food belowground, so take as much with you as you can. Steak is a good choice because it restores lots of hunger points.

46

TIP ⛏

The entrances to caves can often be found on the sides of mountains. Keep an eye out for threats from hostile mobs, as they may be lurking nearby.

MINING TIPS

Now you're ready to head into that cave. No need to panic – if you follow these tips you'll be able to stay safe underground and mine all the ore blocks you could possibly need.

1 Find the entrance to a natural cave – this will lead you down into the ground and is much easier than having to dig your own mine.

2 Place torches on the walls so you can see where you're going and keep an eye out for dangerous mobs.

3 It's easy to get lost underground, but if you always place torches on the same side (e.g., on your left), you can find your way back to the surface when you're finished – just turn around and keep the torches on your opposite side.

4 Never mine the block above your head, as you could end up covered in falling lava. Don't mine the block you're standing on either, as you could fall into a cave full of monsters!

5 Mine every ore block you see – they're rare, very useful for crafting and you'll earn loads of experience points by collecting them.

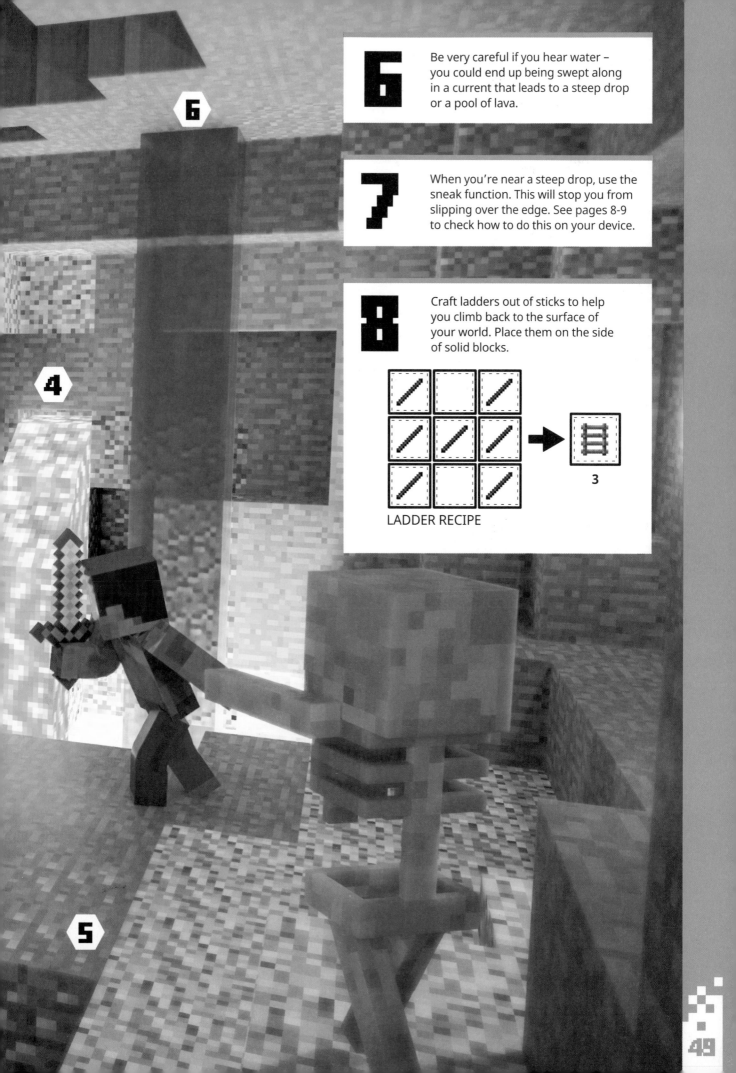

6 Be very careful if you hear water – you could end up being swept along in a current that leads to a steep drop or a pool of lava.

7 When you're near a steep drop, use the sneak function. This will stop you from slipping over the edge. See pages 8-9 to check how to do this on your device.

8 Craft ladders out of sticks to help you climb back to the surface of your world. Place them on the side of solid blocks.

3

LADDER RECIPE

LIFE UNDERGROUND

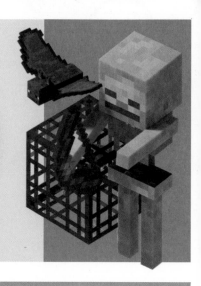

There's a lot more to see underground than stone, ore blocks and hostile mobs. Here are some other things to keep an eye out for when you head beneath the surface of the world.

BATS

Bats spawn in light levels of 3 or lower and like to live in caves. They won't hurt you, but if they take you by surprise you might step over a ledge or into lava. They don't drop anything when defeated. Keep your eyes peeled for them and listen for their squeaks.

WATER

You'll find water underground, too. It flows in streams and forms deep pools in some places.

LAVA

Lava can be found hiding behind stone blocks. It's dangerous and can kill you, so you need to be careful when mining! Underground lavafalls stream down to the bottom of the world, where they form huge lava lakes.

OBSIDIAN

Obsidian can be found near the bottom of the world, where flowing water hits a lava source block. It's the toughest mineable block in Minecraft (bedrock is tougher, but you can't mine it). You won't be able to mine obsidian unless you have a diamond pickaxe. Obsidian can be used to build strong bases, to craft enchantment tables and to build Nether portals so you can get to the Nether.

DUNGEONS

Dungeons are small rooms built out of moss stone and cobblestone. There's a block called a monster spawner in the center of the room – this sinister device produces zombies, skeletons or spiders. You can stop the spawner from producing mobs by placing torches on top of it and on its sides. Dungeons contain up to two loot chests – inside you might find everything from wheat to gold ingots.

GRAVEL

You'll see large amounts of gravel belowground. Unlike most blocks, gravel will fall down if there are no blocks underneath it, and you could easily mine a stone block that's holding up gravel. Be careful – gravel might suffocate you if it falls on top of you, so never mine the block directly over your head. When mined with any tool, it may drop an item called flint. Flint can be used to make arrows (see page 57) and a tool called a flint and steel, which makes fire.

ABANDONED MINE SHAFTS

If you're really lucky, you'll find an abandoned mine shaft underground. Every miner dreams of finding one of these – the hard work has already been done for you, and there are tunnels everywhere just waiting to be explored.

Abandoned mine shafts are a complicated system of tunnels built from wood planks and fence posts.

When you find a cluster of cobwebs, be very careful – there'll be a cave spider spawner inside them and cave spiders nearby.

In some corridors, you'll find mine carts with chests inside them. You'll find valuable items like diamonds, gold ingots and redstone in these chests.

You might find a few torches in abandoned mine shafts.

Inside the tunnels you'll find rails – these are tracks for mine carts.

There are cobwebs all over abandoned mine shafts. If you walk straight into them, you'll get stuck for a few moments.

CAVE SPIDERS

BLOCK HEIGHT

- - - - - - - - - - - - - - - 3

- - - - - - - - - - - - - - - 2

- - - - - - - - - - - - - - - 1

BEHAVIOR
Cave spiders are smaller than regular spiders – they can fit through gaps that are 1 block wide and half a block tall. They are hostile in any light level under 9 and can climb walls.

HOW THEY ATTACK
Cave spiders jump toward you, like regular spiders. Their bites will poison you. The poison lasts for a few seconds and can cause up to 2 health points of damage when playing at the Easy level of Difficulty.

HOW TO DEFEND YOURSELF
Drink a bucket of milk (see page 27) if you've been poisoned – it's like medicine and will get rid of the poison. If you can get close enough, place a torch on top of the cave spider spawner, and a torch on each side of it, too. This will stop it producing more cave spiders.

WHAT THEY DROP
Like regular spiders, cave spiders may also drop string and spider eyes.

ARMOR

Well done – you survived your first mining trip and collected some iron ore!
Now you can craft a set of iron armor, which helps to absorb damage from
things such as mob attacks, lightning, fire and lava.

SMELTING IRON ORE

You need to cook iron ore in
your furnace to turn it into iron
ingots – this is called smelting.
Open up your furnace, then put
coal in the bottom slot and iron
ore blocks in the top slot. After
a few moments of smelting,
an iron ingot will appear in
the output slot. Drag it into
your inventory. Once you have
enough iron ingots, you can craft
these items of armor.

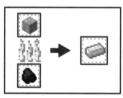

IRON INGOT RECIPE

HELMET

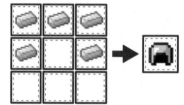

IRON HELMET RECIPE

CHESTPLATE

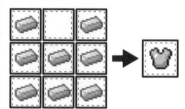

IRON CHESTPLATE RECIPE

BOOTS

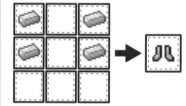

IRON BOOTS RECIPE

LEGGINGS

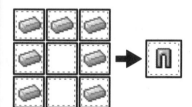

IRON LEGGINGS RECIPE

HOW TO PUT ON YOUR ARMOR

1 Open up your
inventory and look
for your armor
slots. You'll find
that they sit just
to the left of your
skin (character
design) in the top
left corner.

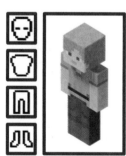

2 Now drag each
separate piece of
armor to the right
armor slot, and
it will appear
on your body.
When you're fully
suited, close your
inventory.

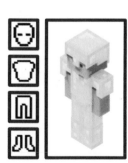

3 An armor bar (found above your
health bar) shows you how much
protection iron armor gives you.
If you were wearing diamond
armor, this bar would be full.

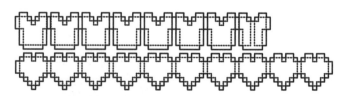

TIP

If you put coal and a gold ore block in your furnace, you can make a gold ingot. By using gold ingots instead of iron ingots, you can follow the recipes shown on page 54 to make a suit of gold armor!

DID YOU KNOW?

You can also make armor from diamond and leather. Diamond is the strongest armor.

TIP

Now is a good time to craft an iron pickaxe. Use the recipe for a stone pickaxe on page 22, but replace the cobblestone with iron ingots.

YOUR NEXT ADVENTURE

Now that you have armor to protect you, you're ready to go on a proper Minecraft adventure farther from home, in exciting new biomes. But before you set off, here are some items you could craft that will help you survive and thrive.

CLOCK

Clocks are useful when you're underground – they tell you whether it's night or day. Wait until daytime to return to the surface, as there will be far fewer dangerous mobs. Craft a clock from redstone and gold ingots.

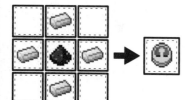

CLOCK RECIPE

COMPASS

This handy item will point to your spawn point. If you find yourself missing home, just select it in your hotbar and follow the red arrow back home. You'll need redstone and iron ingots to craft it.

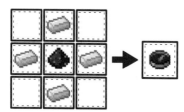

COMPASS RECIPE

PAPER

You'll need paper in your inventory if you want to craft items like banners, books and maps. Track down some sugar canes, then place 3 pieces in your crafting grid to make 3 pieces of paper.

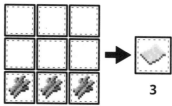

3

PAPER RECIPE

MAP

Maps show you the land that you've explored in your world so that you can easily return to good spots. Select it in your hotbar and hit the "use item" button to start mapping. You'll need a compass and paper.

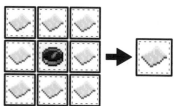

MAP RECIPE

SHIELD

You can use a shield to block attacks from dangerous mobs. They're crafted from any wood planks and an iron ingot. Hold the shield in either hand, then hit the "use item" button to block an attack.

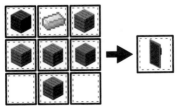

SHIELD RECIPE

BOW

This weapon allows you to shoot arrows at dangerous mobs from a safe distance. You just need sticks and string to craft it. In order to use the bow, you must have at least one arrow in your inventory.

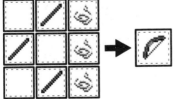

BOW RECIPE

ARROWS

Your bow isn't much use without arrows! You'll just need flint, sticks and feathers to craft them. Chickens may drop feathers if you defeat them, and gravel blocks may drop flint when you mine them.

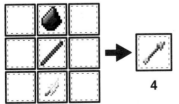

4

ARROWS RECIPE

MINECRAFT DICTIONARY

Hopefully this book has taught you a lot about starting out in Minecraft. But there's so much more to learn! Here's a list of common Minecraft terms you might hear people use and an explanation of what they mean.

BEDROCK

Not to be confused with Bedrock Edition, bedrock is a block found right at the bottom of the world. It's Minecraft's strongest block, and you can't destroy it in Survival mode.

CHUNK

A chunk is an area of the Minecraft world. It's 16 blocks wide, 16 blocks long and 356 blocks high. The Minecraft world generates in chunks around the player. In Creative mode, it's possible to move so quickly that the chunks can't keep up with you and don't appear (or "load") right away.

BOSS MOB

Boss mobs are more dangerous than other mobs – yes, even more dangerous than creepers! There are two boss mobs in Minecraft: the ender dragon and the wither. The ender dragon can only be found in the End dimension, and you'll need to "summon" the wither by building it out of blocks.

GRIEFING

This is the act of causing another player grief. This often involves destroying another player's builds for the sake of annoying them and causing chaos. A person who griefs is called a griefer.

JEB

Jeb (full name Jens Bergensten) is Mojang's lead games developer for Minecraft. He took over this role from Notch (see page 60), the creator of Minecraft, in 2012.

LAG

Lag is a noticeable delay between you pressing buttons to perform an action in your game and that action happening on-screen. It can cause very bad things to happen, e.g., falling off a cliff or failing to defend yourself when under attack from a mob.

MARKETPLACE

Marketplace is Minecraft's in-game store, where you can buy skins, texture packs and fun worlds. Everything is made by community creators.

MELEE

Melee combat refers to close-up, hand-to-hand fighting. If you hit a mob with your sword, that's melee combat. If you shoot them with a bow and arrows, that's not melee combat, as you're attacking from a distance.

MINECON EARTH

MINECON Earth is an annual celebration of Minecraft. Mojang host the event – it's filmed live, then streamed across the world via the Internet so every Minecrafter can watch it.

MOD

Mod is short for modification – it can be anything that changes the way Minecraft looks or behaves. Some mods add new blocks; others change the way blocks and items look.

MOJANG

Mojang is the Swedish videogame developer that created Minecraft. It was founded in 2009 by Notch – the creator of Minecraft. Today, Mojang is owned by Microsoft.

NOOB

A Minecraft noob is a person who has no experience or knowledge of Minecraft. Congratulations – now that you've read this book, you are no longer a noob!

NOTCH

Notch is the games developer who created Minecraft, and he's also the founder of Mojang. His real name is Markus Persson.

PORTAL

A portal is a gateway that lets players travel between the Overworld and one of the other two dimensions in Minecraft. The only way to get to the Nether is to build a Nether portal in the Overworld using obsidian blocks, and activate it using a flint and steel. The only way to get to the End is to find an End portal in an Overworld stronghold and activate it with items called eyes of ender. Be warned – the Nether and the End are extremely dangerous, so you'll need to be prepared!

PEACEFUL

Remember right at the beginning of this book we suggested you change the Difficulty setting to Easy? Well, another option for Survival mode is Peaceful Difficulty. Peaceful is a bit like Creative mode – mobs won't attack you and you won't need to worry about eating, but you will still need to gather resources and craft items to survive.

REALMS

Realms are official Minecraft servers that let you set up a private world so you and your friends can play together. They're online and always accessible, even when you log off. They're completely safe – only people you invite can join your Realm. What you do there is up to you!

SANDBOX

This is a style of game in which players can do what they like. There's no set path through the game, or set levels to complete. Minecraft is a sandbox game – you can choose how to play and what kind of adventure you want to have.

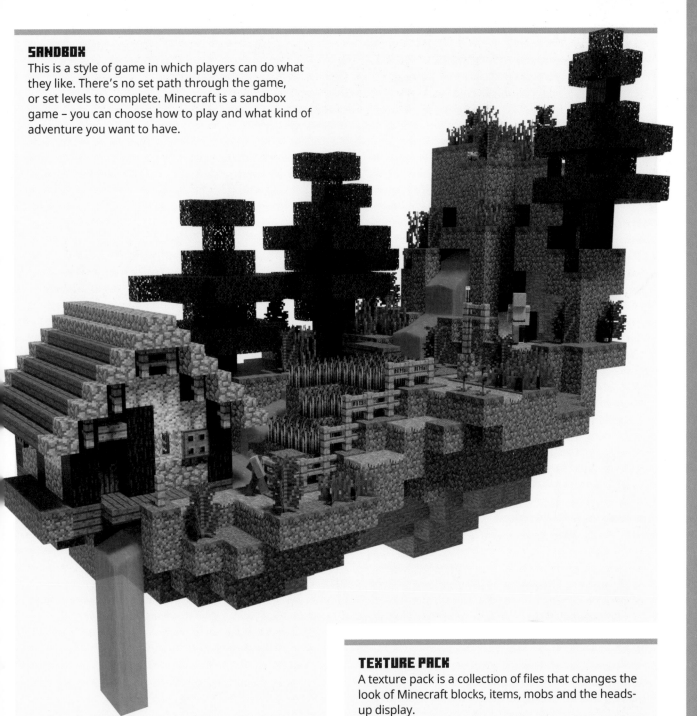

TEXTURE PACK

A texture pack is a collection of files that changes the look of Minecraft blocks, items, mobs and the heads-up display.

SEED

Every Minecraft world you create has a seed – a string of numbers and letters a bit like a barcode. If you create a really cool world, you can share the seed with your friends and they'll be able to create the exact same world on their own device. To check your seed, open your game then go to the settings menu. Keep scrolling down until you see the section labeled "seed." If you want to use a specific seed, just add it into the seed section when you set up your world.

UPDATES

Minecraft is never finished – the developers are always coming up with exciting new things to add to the game and releasing them in groups, as updates. Updates usually have names – e.g., the Update Aquatic. Sometimes updates are used to remove things as well.

VANILLA MINECRAFT

Vanilla Minecraft is the original version of the game – the version that hasn't been changed in any way. In this book, we've been playing vanilla Minecraft because we haven't used any mods to change the way the game looks or works.

SERVER

A server is an online world where you can play Minecraft together with your friends.

GOODBYE!

Wow, there's a new gleam in your eye! You've become an expert Minecraft player! We hope you've had fun while you've been reading this book.

We also hope you're already thinking about how you can use what you've learned to go on new adventures of your own. Minecraft is all about your journey.

There's no right way to play, other than your way, and whether you want to explore, build, invent or battle, there are lots of ways to do them!

Go forth and make Minecraft yours!

ALEX WILTSHIRE
THE MOJANG TEAM

STAY IN THE KNOW!

GUIDE TO:
☑ CREATIVE

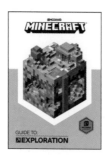
GUIDE TO:
☑ EXPLORATION

GUIDE TO:
☐ THE NETHER & THE END

GUIDE TO:
☑ REDSTONE

GUIDE TO:
☑ ENCHANTMENTS & POTIONS

GUIDE TO:
☑ PVP MINIGAMES

GUIDE TO:
☑ FARMING

THEME PARK ADVENTURE

INTO THE GAME!

NIGHT OF THE BATS!

Learn about the latest Minecraft books when you sign up for our newsletter at **ReadMinecraft.com**

DEL REY

RANDOM HOUSE CHILDREN'S BOOKS

MOJANG

™ & © 2019 Mojang Synergies AB. All rights reserved.